T0375529

BIBLICAL WISDOM
for
MONEY MANAGEMENT

Understanding God's Financial Truths

G R E G   H U B E R

WESTBOW
P R E S S®
A DIVISION OF THOMAS NELSON
& ZONDERVAN

WestBow Press books may be ordered through booksellers or by contacting:

WestBow Press
A Division of Thomas Nelson & Zondervan
1663 Liberty Drive
Bloomington, IN 47403
www.westbowpress.com
844-714-3454

ISBN: 979-8-3850-2060-7 (sc)
ISBN: 979-8-3850-2062-1 (e)

Library of Congress Control Number: 2024904920

Print information available on the last page.

WestBow Press rev. date: 05/13/2024

The NASB 2020 uses italics to communicate to the reader words that are not found in the original language but are implied in the original language or are needed for a complete thought in English.

Verses in the Bible that are quoting someone speaking include the quote in quotation marks. If the person speaking is not stated in the verse, then this is noted in brackets under the verse, or passage of multiple verses. These verses are oftentimes excerpts from longer speeches.

CONTENTS

INTRODUCTION

What the Bible teaches about managing money is important to *all* Christians regardless of income, wealth, and financial well-being. The Bible also provides wisdom that is beneficial to non-Christians. Simply put, understanding the Bible's teachings will help you to make better financial decisions and be more content!

The book includes 345 Bible verses in 163 different passages and is organized into chapters focused on different topics. There are roughly an equal number of passages from the Old Testament and New Testament. And the passages from the New Testament include some of Jesus's parables. The Bible clearly has a *lot* to say!

The Bible also clearly states that Scripture is for teaching, reproof, correction, and training in righteousness. This applies to Christians as they seek to apply Biblical wisdom to how they manage money.

"All Scripture is inspired by God and beneficial for teaching, for rebuke, for correction, and for training in righteousness; so that the man *or woman* of God may be fully capable, equipped for every good work" (2 Timothy 3:16–17).

This book is intended to help you understand what the Bible teaches about the key aspects of money management. I encourage you to spend time studying and reflecting on what the Bible teaches.

Questions are provided at the end of each chapter in case you want to use it as a Bible study. This section can also be used to make notes.

If you are married or engaged to be married, it is very important for both of you to study what the Bible says, so you can ensure you are both in agreement regarding how to manage your money. The goals and priorities you set related to managing money will be very important to your relationship over time. Disagreements about money have, unfortunately, been shown to be one of the top contributors to marital stress and divorce.

Educational articles on practical applications (e.g., giving, budgeting, debt, retirement saving, education saving, buying a home, investing, estate planning, etc.) are not included in this book. There are other resources for this, some of which agree and others disagree. And recommendations for practical applications can change over time. What the Bible teaches is timeless.

Chapter 1

OWNERSHIP

Attitudes toward money are shaped by your belief system, and these attitudes will significantly impact your priorities and behaviors as they relate to the uses of money (e.g., giving, saving, and spending). A key first step is to consider what the Bible says regarding who is the creator and how this affects your beliefs regarding ownership of the resources you have.

BIBLE VERSES	
Exodus 19:5	Now then, if you will indeed obey My voice and keep My covenant, then you shall be My own possession among all the peoples, for all the earth is Mine. *[God is speaking]*
Deuteronomy 10:14	"Behold, to the LORD your God belong heaven and the highest heavens, the earth and all that is in it." *[Moses is speaking.]*

1 Chronicles 29:11–13 (ESV)	"Yours, O Lord, is the greatness and the power and the glory and the victory and the majesty, for all that is in the heavens and in the earth is yours. Yours is the kingdom, O Lord, and you are exalted as head above all. Both riches and honor come from you, and you rule over all. In your hand are power and might, and in your hand it is to make great and to give strength to all. And now we thank you, our God, and praise your glorious name." [*David is speaking.*]
Nehemiah 9:6 (ESV)	"You are the Lord, you alone. You have made heaven, the heaven of heavens, with all their host, the earth and all that is on it, the seas and all that is in them; and you preserve all of them; and the host of heaven worships you." [*A group of eight Levites is speaking.*]
Job 41:11	"Who has been first *to give* to Me, that I should repay *him*? *Whatever* is under the entire heaven is Mine." [*God is speaking.*]
Psalm 24:1–2	The earth is the Lord's and all it contains, the world, and those who live in it. For He has founded it upon the seas and established it upon the rivers.
Psalm 50:10–12	"For every animal of the forest is Mine, the cattle on a thousand hills. I know every bird of the mountains, and everything that moves in the field is Mine. If I were hungry I would not tell you, for

	the world is Mine, and everything it contains." *[God is speaking.]*
Psalm 89:11	The heavens are Yours, the earth is also Yours; the world and all it contains, You have established them all.
Acts 17:24–25	"The God who made the world and everything that is in it, since He is Lord of heaven and earth, does not dwell in temples made by hands; nor is He served by human hands, as though He needed anything, since He Himself gives to all *people* life and breath and all things." *[Paul is speaking.]*
1 Corinthians 10:26 (ESV)	For "the earth is the Lord's, and the fullness thereof." *[Paul is citing Psalm 24:1.]*
Colossians 1:15–17	He is the image of the invisible God, the firstborn of all creation: for by Him all things were created, *both* in the heavens and on earth, visible and invisible, whether thrones, or dominions, or rulers, or authorities—all things have been created through Him and for Him. He is before all things, and in Him all things hold together.
Revelation 4:11	"Worthy are You, our Lord and our God, to receive glory and honor and power; for You created all things, and because of Your will they existed, and were created." *[Twenty-four elders around God's throne are speaking.]*

REAL-LIFE APPLICATION

As a scientist, Joe was looking for evidence of God's creative power. The first thing he considered was the immense size of the universe. Hubble telescope observations led to estimates of one hundred–two hundred billion galaxies. And our galaxy, the Milky Way, is estimated to have two hundred billion stars. The second thing he considered was the very existence of life on Earth, including some of this life being sentient (e.g., having feelings and being responsive to its environment) and some also being sapient (e.g., self-aware, intelligent, and capable of higher reasoning). The third thing he considered was the incredible complexity of the human body, with approximately one hundred billion neurons in the brain and one hundred trillion bacteria and other microbial cells in the digestive system. He concluded that all of these are hard to explain without God as the creative force.

QUESTIONS

1. Do you recognize God as the creator of the universe and life on Earth? Why or why not? And if not, then who or what do you think is responsible?

2. Are you thankful to God for your life? If yes, what is your response? Does this affect how you view money?

Chapter 2

STEWARDSHIP

Closely related to ownership is stewardship, as a steward is responsible for using money in the way in which the owner intends. Once you have concluded what the Bible says about ownership, the next step is to ascertain whether you are being a good steward.

BIBLE VERSES	
Matthew 6:24	"No one can serve two masters; for either he will hate the one and love the other, or he will be devoted to one and despise the other. You cannot serve God and wealth." [*Jesus is speaking.*]
Matthew 25: 19–30 (ESV)	"Now after a long time the master of those servants came and settled accounts with them. And he who had received the five talents came forward, bringing five talents more, saying, 'Master, you delivered to me five talents; here, I have made five talents more.' His master said to him, 'Well done, good and faithful servant. You have been faithful over a little; I will set you over much. Enter into the joy of

5

	your master.' And he also who had the two talents came forward, saying, 'Master, you delivered to me two talents; here, I have made two talents more.' His master said to him, 'Well done, good and faithful servant. You have been faithful over a little; I will set you over much. Enter into the joy of your master.' He also who had received the one talent came forward, saying, 'Master, I knew you to be a hard man, reaping where you did not sow, and gathering where you scattered no seed, so I was afraid, and I went and hid your talent in the ground. Here, you have what is yours.' But his master answered him, 'You wicked and slothful servant! You knew that I reap where I have not sown and gather where I scattered no seed? Then you ought to have invested my money with the bankers, and at my coming I should have received what was my own with interest. So take the talent from him and give it to him who has the ten talents. For to everyone who has more will be given, and he will have an abundance. But from the one who has not, even what he has will be taken away. And cast the worthless servant into the outer darkness. In that place there will be weeping and gnashing of teeth.'" [*Jesus is speaking.*]
Luke 12:42–48 (ESV)	And the Lord said, "Who then is the faithful and wise manager, whom his master will set over his household, to give them their portion of food at the proper time? Blessed is that

	servant whom his master will find so doing when he comes. Truly, I say to you, he will set him over all his possessions. But if that servant says to himself, 'My master is delayed in coming,' and begins to beat the male and female servants, and to eat and drink and get drunk, the master of that servant will come on a day when he does not expect him and at an hour he does not know, and will cut him in pieces and put him with the unfaithful. And that servant who knew his master's will but did not get ready or act according to his will, will receive a severe beating. But the one who did not know, and did what deserved a beating, will receive a light beating. Everyone to whom much was given, of him much will be required, and from him to whom they entrusted much, they will demand the more."
Luke 16:10–13 (ESV)	"One who is faithful in a very little is also faithful in much, and one who is dishonest in a very little is also dishonest in much. If then you have not been faithful in the unrighteous wealth, who will entrust to you the true riches? And if you have not been faithful in that which is another's, who will give you that which is your own? No servant can serve two masters, for either he will hate the one and love the other, or he will be devoted to one and despise the other. You cannot serve God and money." [*Jesus is speaking.*]

1 Corinthians 4:2	In this case, moreover, it is required of stewards that one be found trustworthy.

REAL-LIFE APPLICATION

Serenity had saved a significant amount of money for a home downpayment by the time she was in her mid-thirties but felt convicted that the Lord was telling her to give this money to someone in need. So she did so, realizing that it was really his money. While she was not expecting this, the Lord led a wealthy person from her church who heard about her faithfulness to replace the money she had given away.

QUESTIONS

1. What are your current priorities for the use of money (giving, saving, and spending)? Do you think that these priorities and uses reflect good stewardship? If not, then what changes should you make?

2. How would you respond if you felt the Lord telling you to give away money that you had been saving for a specific purpose? List examples if you have had this experience.

3. Do you seek the Lord's guidance regarding how you use your money? If not, why not?

4. Do you agree that it is hard to both desire money and possessions for yourself and be a good steward of what God has blessed you with? Have you ever felt stress related to this?

Chapter 3

TITHING

Perhaps the first practical topic related to stewardship is tithing. The practice of tithing started with Abraham, continued through the Old Testament, and was mentioned by Jesus. And it is clear in the New Testament that those who preach and teach the gospel are to be financially supported by those who are being taught.

BIBLE VERSES	
Genesis 14:18–20 (ESV)	And Melchizedek king of Salem brought out bread and wine. (He was priest of God Most High.) And he blessed him and said, "Blessed be Abram by God Most High, Possessor of heaven and earth; and blessed be God Most High, who has delivered your enemies into your hand!" And Abram gave him a tenth of everything.
Leviticus 27:30–33	"Now all the tithe of the land, of the seed of the land *or* of the fruit of the tree, is the LORD's; it is holy to the LORD. If, therefore, someone should ever *want* to redeem part of his tithe, he shall add to it a fifth of it. For every tenth part of herd or flock, whatever passes under the rod,

	the tenth one shall be holy to the LORD. He is not to be concerned whether *it is* good or bad, nor shall he exchange it; yet if he does exchange it, then both it and its substitute shall become holy. It shall not be redeemed." [*God is speaking.*]
Numbers 18:21	"To the sons of Levi, behold, I have given all the tithe in Israel as an inheritance, in return for their service which they perform, the service of the tent of meeting." [*God is speaking.*]
2 Chronicles 31:4–5	Also he told the people who lived in Jerusalem to give the portion due to the priests and the Levites, so that they might devote themselves to the Law of the LORD. As soon as the order spread, the sons of Israel abundantly provided the first fruits of grain, new wine, oil, honey, and of all the produce of the field; and they brought in abundantly the tithe of everything.
Nehemiah 13:10–12	I also discovered that the portions of the Levites had not been given *to them*, so the Levites and the singers who performed the service had gone away, each to his own field. So I reprimanded the officials and said, "Why has the house of God been neglected?" Then I gathered them together and stationed them at their posts. All Judah then brought the tithe of the grain, wine, and oil into the storehouses. [*Nehemiah is speaking*]

Proverbs 3:9–10	Honor the LORD from your wealth, and from the first of all your produce; then your barns will be filled with plenty, and your vats will overflow with new wine.
Malachi 3:8–11 (ESV)	"Will man rob God? Yet you are robbing me! But you say, 'How have we robbed You?' In your tithes and contributions. You are cursed with a curse, for you are robbing me, the whole nation of you. Bring the full tithe into the storehouse, that there may be food in my house. And thereby put me to the test, says the LORD of hosts, if I will not open the windows of heaven for you and pour down for you a blessing until there is no more need. I will rebuke the devourer for you, so that it will not destroy the fruits of your soil, and your vine in the field shall not fail to bear, says the LORD of hosts." *[God is speaking.]*
Matthew 23:23	"Woe to you, scribes and Pharisees, hypocrites! For you tithe mint and dill and cumin, and have neglected the weightier provisions of the Law: justice and mercy and faithfulness; but these *are the things* you should have done without neglecting the others." *[Jesus is speaking.]*
Galatians 6:6	The one who is taught the word is to share all good things with the one who teaches *him*.

1 Timothy 5:17–18 (ESV)	Let the elders who rule well be considered worthy of double honor, especially those who labor in preaching and teaching. For the Scripture says "You shall not muzzle an ox when it treads out the grain," and, "The laborer deserves his wages." *[Scriptures are Deuteronomy 25:4 and Luke 10:7]*

REAL-LIFE APPLICATION

Elijah was personally involved with a local Christian para-church ministry and was considering directing all his giving to this ministry. However, after reviewing Scripture, he realized that he should first be tithing to his local church. After all, his church could not function without the financial support of its members. He ultimately decided to give a tithe to the church and give money in excess of his tithe to the local para-church ministry. He also continued to give his time to the work of the para-church ministry.

QUESTIONS

1. Tithing in biblical times was based primarily on the increase people received in the form of crops and livestock, as this was the basis for the economy in these times. This increase was a reflection of God's blessings, and they were to tithe based on this. What do you think is the equivalent today, and why?
    -   Income from working?
    -   Income from investments?
    -   Appreciation in investments?
    -   Inheritances?
    -   All of the above?
    -   Other? (specify below)

2. Do you think tithing is still relevant today? If yes, do you currently tithe or do you have a plan for doing so? If no, why not?

3. Do you think tithes should go entirely to churches? If not, why not?

4. If you give to your church, whether it is a tithe or not, what is your motivation for doing so?

Chapter 4

GENEROSITY

While tithing is considered by some to be a command, the Bible is clear that generosity is a much broader calling for Christians. The primary focus is on the willingness to give.

BIBLE VERSES	
Deuteronomy 12:6–7	"You shall bring there your burnt offerings, your sacrifices, your tithes, the contribution of your hand, your vowed offerings, your voluntary offerings, and the firstborn of your herd and of your flock. There you and your households shall eat before the LORD your God, and rejoice in all your undertakings in which the LORD your God has blessed you." [*Moses is speaking.*]
Deuteronomy 16:17	"Everyone shall give as he is able, in accordance with the blessing of the LORD your God which He has given you." [*Moses is speaking.*]

1 Chronicles 29:9	Then the people rejoiced because they had offered so willingly, for they made their offering to the LORD wholeheartedly, and King David also rejoiced greatly.
Psalm 37:21	The wicked borrows and does not pay back, but the righteous is gracious and gives.
Proverbs 11:25	A generous person will be prosperous, and one who gives *others* plenty of water will himself be given plenty.
Matthew 6:19–21	"Do not store up for yourselves treasures on earth, where moth and rust destroy, and where thieves break in and steal. But store up for yourselves treasure in heaven, where neither moth nor rust destroys, and where thieves do not break in or steal; for where your treasure is, there your heart will be also." [*Jesus is speaking.*]
Matthew 7:12	"In everything, therefore, treat people the same way you want them to treat you, for this is the Law and the Prophets." [*Jesus is speaking.*]
Matthew 22:36–40 (ESV)	"Teacher, which is the great commandment in the Law?" And he said to him, "You shall love the Lord your God with all your heart and with all your soul and with all your mind. This is the great and first commandment. And a second is like it: You shall love your neighbor as yourself.

	On these two commandments depend all the Law and the Prophets." [*A Pharisee is speaking with Jesus.*]
Mark 12:41–44 (ESV)	And he sat down opposite the treasury and watched the people putting money into the offering box. Many rich people put in large sums. And a poor widow came and put in two small copper coins, which make a penny. And he called his disciples to him and said to them, "Truly I say to you, this poor widow has put in more than all those who are contributing to the offering box. For they all contributed out of their abundance, but she out of her poverty has put in everything she had, all she had to live on." [*Jesus is speaking.*]
Luke 6:38	"Give, and it will be given to you. They will pour into your lap a good measure—pressed down, shaken together, *and* running over. For by your standard of measure it will be measured to you in return." [*Jesus is speaking.*]
Acts 20:35	"In everything I showed you that by working hard in this way you must help the weak and remember the words of the Lord Jesus, that He Himself said, 'It is more blessed to give than to receive.'" [*Paul is speaking.*]

2 Corinthians 8:1–4 (ESV)	We want you to know, brothers, about the grace of God that has been given among the churches of Macedonia, for in a severe test of affliction, their abundance of joy and their extreme poverty have overflowed in a wealth of generosity on their part. For they gave according to their means, as I can testify, and beyond their means, of their own accord, begging us earnestly for the favor of taking part in the relief of the saints.
2 Corinthians 9:6–11 (ESV)	The point is this: whoever sows sparingly will also reap sparingly, and whoever sows bountifully will also reap bountifully. Each one must give as he has decided in his heart, not reluctantly or under compulsion, for God loves a cheerful giver. And God is able to make all grace abound to you, so that having all sufficiency in all things at all times, you may abound in every good work. As is it written, "He has distributed freely, he has given to the poor, his righteousness endures forever." He who supplies seed to the sower and bread for food will supply and multiply your seed for sowing and increase the harvest of your righteousness. You will be enriched in every way to be generous in every way, which through us will produce thanksgiving to God. *[Paul quoting Psalm 112:9]*
Philippians 4:16–19	For even in Thessalonica you sent a *gift* more than once for my needs. Not that I seek the gift *itself*, but I seek the profit which increases to your account. But I have received everything

	in full and have an abundance; I am amply supplied, having received from Epaphroditus what you have sent, a fragrant aroma, an acceptable sacrifice, pleasing to God. And my God will supply all your needs according to His riches in glory in Christ Jesus.
1 Timothy 6:17–19	Instruct those who are rich in this present world not to be conceited or to set their hope on the uncertainty of riches, but on God, who richly supplies us with all things to enjoy. *Instruct them* to do good, to be rich in good works, to be generous and ready to share, storing up for themselves the treasure of a good foundation for the future, so that they may take hold of that which is truly life.
Hebrews 13:2	Do not neglect hospitality to strangers, for by this some have entertained angels without knowing it.
Hebrews 13:16	And do not neglect doing good and sharing, for with such sacrifices God is pleased.

REAL-LIFE APPLICATION

When Angela returned from a mission trip to Uganda her grandparents were moved by the work of the ministry she served with, as they were helping young homeless boys on the streets of Kampala get food and were also taking many of them to a camp in the country where they would be properly cared for and get an education. Her grandparents gave thousands of dollars to the ministry for the purchase of land and goats. These were important in enabling them to give the boys experience with raising crops and animals, both of which are common occupations in Uganda.

QUESTIONS

1. What is your general attitude toward giving money? Are you eager or reluctant to do so? Does it bring you joy?

2. Which statement below most closely represents your view on giving?
   - I don't have enough income to give.
   - I give what I have left over after my expenses.
   - I focus on tithing and don't give more than this.
   - I give more than what is required by a tithe.
   - I plan what I truly need and give away the rest.
   - I give of my time instead of giving money.
   - I give both my time and money

3. Where are you currently giving money and how much of your income does that represent? What percentage of your income do you think you could give away if you pushed yourself?

4. Are there ways in which you could be more generous to your neighbors, even if not financially?

Chapter 5

CARING FOR THE POOR

Closely related to generosity is caring for the poor. It is clear in the Bible that this is important to God.

BIBLE VERSES	
Leviticus 19:10	"And you shall not glean your vineyard, nor shall you gather the fallen grapes of your vineyard; you shall leave them for the needy and for the stranger. I am the LORD your God." [*God is speaking.*]
Deuteronomy 15:7–11	"If there is a poor person among you, one of your brothers, in any of your towns in your land which the LORD your God is giving you, you shall not harden your heart, nor close your hand from your poor brother; but you shall fully open your hand to him, and generously lend him enough for his need *in* whatever he lacks. Be careful that there is no mean-spirited thought in your heart, such as, 'The seventh year, the year of release of debts, is near,' and your eye is malicious toward your poor brother,

	and you give him nothing; then he may cry out to the LORD against you, and it will be a sin in you. You shall generously give to him, and your heart shall not be grudging when you give to him, because for this thing the LORD your God will bless you in all your work, and in all your undertakings. For the poor will not cease to exist in the land; therefore I am commanding you, saying, 'You shall fully open your hand to your brother, to your needy and poor in your land.'" [*Moses is speaking.*]
Deuteronomy 24:19–21	"When you reap your harvest in your field and forget a sheaf in the field, you are not to go back and get it; it shall belong to the stranger, the orphan, and to the widow, in order that the LORD your God may bless you in all the work of your hands. When you beat *the olives* off your olive tree, you are not to search through the branches again; *that* shall be *left* for the stranger, the orphan, and for the widow. When you gather the grapes of your vineyard, you are not to go over it again; *that* shall be *left* for the stranger, the orphan, and the widow." [*Moses is speaking.*]
Proverbs 14:21	One who despises his neighbor sins, but one who is gracious to the poor is blessed.
Proverbs 14:31	One who oppresses the poor taunts his Maker, but one who is gracious to the needy honors Him.

Proverbs 19:17	One who is gracious to a poor person lends to the LORD, and He will repay him for his good deed.
Proverbs 21:13	One who shuts his ear to the outcry of the poor will also call out himself, and not be answered.
Proverbs 22:9	One who is generous will be blessed, because he gives some of his food to the poor.
Proverbs 22:16	One who oppresses the poor to make more for himself, *or* gives to the rich, *will* only *come* to poverty.
Proverbs 28:27	One who gives to the poor will never lack *anything*, but one who shuts his eyes will have many curses.
Ezekiel 16:49	"Behold, this was the guilt of your sister Sodom: she and her daughters had arrogance, plenty of food, and carefree ease, but she did not help the poor and needy." [*God is speaking.*]
Matthew 6:3–4	"But when you give to the poor, do not let your left hand know what your right hand is doing, so that your charitable giving will be in secret; and your Father who sees *what is done* in secret will reward you." [*Jesus is speaking.*]
Matthew 19:21–26	Jesus said to him, "If you want to be complete, go *and* sell your possessions and give to *the* poor, and you will have treasure in heaven; and come,

	follow Me." But when the young man heard this statement, he went away grieving; for he was one who owned much property. And Jesus said to His disciples, "Truly I say to you, it will be hard for a rich person to enter the kingdom of heaven. And again I say to you, it is easier for a camel to go through the eye of a needle, than for a rich person to enter the kingdom of God." When the disciples heard *this*, they were very astonished and said, "Then who can be saved?" And looking at *them*, Jesus said to them, "With people this is impossible, but with God all things are possible."
Matthew 25:34–40 (ESV)	"Then the King will say to those on his right, 'Come, you who are blessed by my Father, inherit the kingdom prepared for you from the foundation of the world. For I was hungry and you gave me food, I was thirsty and you gave me drink, I was a stranger and you welcomed me, I was naked and you clothed me, I was sick and you visited me, I was in prison and you came to me.' Then the righteous will answer him, saying, 'Lord, when did we see you hungry and feed you, or thirsty and give you drink? And when did we see you a stranger and welcome you, or naked and clothe you? And when did we see you sick or in prison and visit you?' And the King will answer them, 'Truly, I say to you, as you did it to one of the least of these my brothers, you did it to me.'" *[Jesus is speaking.]*

Luke 10:36–37	"Which of these three do you think proved to be a neighbor to the man who fell into the robbers' *hands*?" And he said, "The one who showed compassion to him." Then Jesus said to him, "Go and do the same." [*Jesus speaking with a lawyer.*]
Luke 14:12–14	Now He also went on to say to the one who had invited Him, "Whenever you give a luncheon or a dinner, do not invite your friends, your brothers, your relatives, nor wealthy neighbors, otherwise they may also invite you *to a meal* in return, and *that* will be your repayment. But whenever you give a banquet, invite people who are poor, who have disabilities, who are limping, *and* people who are blind; and you will be blessed, since they do not have *the means* to repay you; for you will be repaid at the resurrection of the righteous." [*Jesus is speaking.*]
James 1:27	Pure and undefiled religion in the sight of *our* God and Father is this: to visit orphans and widows in their distress, *and* to keep oneself unstained by the world.
1 John 3:16–18	We know love by this, that He laid down His life for us; and we ought to lay down our lives for the brothers *and sisters*. But whoever has worldly goods and sees his brother *or sister* in need, and closes his heart against him, how does the love of God remain in him? Little children, let's not love with word or with tongue, but in deed and truth.

REAL-LIFE APPLICATION

Marie met Andre, a construction worker who had come to the United States to find work and was living with his wife and four children. He was a skilled and hard worker but knew very limited English and had a hard time finding work. Marie helped him to understand how to get the services his family needed, arranged to get them furnishings for the place they were living, helped them to get free food from a local food bank, and loaned them money. This was greatly appreciated by Andre and his family and led to a long-term relationship that is treasured by both of them.

QUESTIONS

1. The Bible directs people to take a variety of actions to care for the poor (below). Which are relevant today and which ones could you participate in? Be specific below.
   1. Lending them money
   2. Leaving things for them to glean
   3. Giving food, drink, shelter, and/or clothing
   4. Visiting them in order to encourage them
   5. Contributing to ministries that help them
   6. Others

2. How does the Bible caution those who are capable of caring for the poor but choose not to do so?

3. When you have furniture, clothing, or other items you don't need do you consider donating them to a thrift shop instead of selling them online to make some money?

4. When you think of helping people who are poor and in need do you prioritize those in your local community or elsewhere in the world? Why is this your priority?

Chapter 6

PLANNING AND BUDGETING

Successful planning takes wisdom, discernment, discipline, and the advice of wise counselors. It is important to understand the biblical principles underlying the creation of financial goals, plans, and budgets.

BIBLE VERSES	
Genesis 41:34–36	"Let Pharaoh take action to appoint overseers in charge of the land, and let him take a fifth *of the produce* of the land of Egypt *as a tax* in the seven years of abundance. Then have them collect all the food of these good years that are coming, and store up the grain for food in the cities under Pharaoh's authority, and have them guard *it*. Let the food be *used* as a reserve for the land for the seven years of famine which will occur in the land of Egypt, so that the land will not perish during the famine." *[Joseph is speaking.]*

Proverbs 3:13–16	Blessed is a person who finds wisdom, and one who obtains understanding. For her profit is better than the profit of silver and her produce better than gold. She is more precious than jewels, and nothing you desire compares to her. Long life is in her right hand; in her left hand are riches and honor.
Proverbs 19:21	Many plans are in a person's heart, but the advice of the LORD will stand.
Proverbs 21:5	The plans of the diligent certainly *lead* to advantage, but everyone who is in a hurry certainly *comes* to poverty.
Proverbs 21:20	There is precious treasure and oil in the home of the wise, but a foolish person swallows it up.
Proverbs 24:3–4	By wisdom a house is built, and by understanding it is established; and by knowledge the rooms are filled with precious and pleasant riches.
Proverbs 24:27	Prepare your work outside, and make it ready for yourself in the field; afterward, then, build your house.
Proverbs 27:23–24	Know well the condition of your flocks, *and* pay attention to your herds; for riches are not forever, nor does a crown *endure* to all generations.
Matthew 7:24–27	"Therefore, everyone who hears these words of Mine, and acts on them, will be like a wise man who built his house on the rock. And the rain

	fell and the floods came, and the winds blew and slammed against that house; and *yet* it did not fall, for it had been founded on the rock. And everyone who hears these words of Mine, and does not act on them, will be like a foolish man who built his house on the sand. And the rain fell and the floods came, and the winds blew and slammed against that house; and it fell—and its collapse was great." [*Jesus is speaking.*]
Luke 14:28–30	"For which one of you, when he wants to build a tower, does not first sit down and calculate the cost, *to see* if he has *enough* to complete *it*? Otherwise, when he has laid a foundation and is not able to finish, all who are watching *it* will begin to ridicule him, saying, 'This person began to build, and was not able to finish!'" [*Jesus is speaking.*]
Romans 13:7	Pay to all what is due to them: tax to whom tax is *due*; custom to whom custom; respect to whom respect; honor to whom honor.
Colossians 3:23	Whatever you do, do your work heartily as for the Lord and not for people.
	Verses Related to Family
Proverbs 13:22	A good person leaves an inheritance to his grandchildren, and the wealth of a sinner is stored up for the righteous.

Proverbs 19:14	House and wealth are an inheritance from fathers, but a prudent wife is from the LORD.
2 Corinthians 12:14	Here for this third time I am ready to come to you, and I will not be a burden to you; for I do not seek what is yours, but you; for children are not responsible to save up for *their* parents, but parents for *their* children.
1 Timothy 5:3–4	Honor widows who are actually widows; but if any widow has children or grandchildren, they must first learn to show proper respect for their own family and to give back compensation to their parents; for this is acceptable in the sight of God.
1 Timothy 5:8	But if anyone does not provide for his own, and especially for those of his household, he has denied the faith and is worse than an unbeliever.
1 Timothy 5:16	If any woman who is a believer has *dependent* widows, she must assist them and the church must not be burdened, so that it may assist those who are actually widows.
	Verses about Having Counselors
Proverbs 5:23	He will die for lack of instruction, and in the greatness of his foolishness he will go astray.
Proverbs 11:14	Where there is no guidance the people fall, but in an abundance of counselors there is victory.

Proverbs 15:22	Without consultation, plans are frustrated, but with many counselors they succeed.
	Verses about Ants Being Wise
Proverbs 6:6–8	Go to the ant, you lazy one, observe its ways and be wise, which, having no chief, officer, or ruler, prepares its food in the summer *and* gathers its provision in the harvest.
Proverbs 30:24–25	Four things are small on the earth, but they are exceedingly wise: the ants are not a strong people, but they prepare their food in the summer.

APPLICATION

Dave and Sally had saved diligently for retirement and were now retired and living comfortably. They knew they had saved enough to provide an inheritance for their adult children but wanted to spend more time with the children and grandchildren. A financial planning analysis showed that they could fund vacations for the entire family every two years and still provide an inheritance. They are now enjoying making memories with their family!

QUESTIONS

1. What are short-term and long-term biblical examples of goal setting and planning? And the consequences of poor planning? Have you ever experienced the consequences of poor planning?

2. What are your goals in managing your money and what do you need long-term plans for? Do you know the "condition of your flocks" as it relates to money?

3. Is providing for your family a priority as you decide how you will use money? Is this true long-term as well as short-term? Are you planning to leave an inheritance?

4. What does the Bible say about the importance of advisors? Does someone give you advice regarding financial planning and important financial decisions? If not, then why don't you do this?

5. Why do you think the analogy regarding ants was included in the Bible

Chapter 7

DEBT AND LENDING

While not expressed as a sin, the Bible is clear that debt is to be avoided, including cosigning on a debt that someone else owes. And if a person is in debt, that it should be a priority to get out of debt. Interestingly, the Bible also has verses that encourage lending under the right circumstances.

BIBLE VERSES	
Deuteronomy 28:12	"The LORD will open for you His good storehouse, the heavens, to give rain to your land in its season and to bless every work of your hand; and you will lend to many nations, but you will not borrow." [*Moses is speaking.*]
2 Kings 4:1–7 (ESV)	Now the wife of one of the sons of the prophets cried to Elisha, "Your servant my husband is dead, and you know that your servant feared the LORD, but the creditor has come to take my two children to be his slaves." And Elisha said to her, "What shall I do for you? Tell me; what have you in the house?" And she said, "Your

	servant has nothing in the house except a jar of oil." Then he said, "Go outside, borrow vessels from all your neighbors, empty vessels and not too few. Then go in and shut the door behind yourself and your sons, and pour into all these vessels. And when one is full, set it aside." So she went from him and shut the door behind herself and her sons. And as she poured they brought the vessels to her. When the vessels were full, she said to her son, "Bring me another vessel." And he said to her, "There is not another." Then the oil stopped flowing. She came and told the man of God, and he said, "Go, sell the oil and pay your debts, and you and your sons can live on the rest."
Proverbs 22:7	The rich rules over the poor, and the borrower *becomes* the lender's slave.
Romans 13:8	Owe nothing to anyone except to love one another; for the one who loves his neighbor has fulfilled *the* Law.
	Verses about Cosigning
Proverbs 6:1–5	My son, if you have become a guarantor for your neighbor, *or* have given a handshake for a stranger, *if* you have been ensnared by the words of your mouth, *or* caught by the words of your mouth, then do this, my son, and save yourself: since you have come into the hand of your neighbor, go, humble yourself, and be urgent with your neighbor *to free yourself.*

	Give no sleep to your eyes, nor slumber to your eyelids; save yourself like a gazelle from *the hunter's* hand, and like a bird from the hand of the fowler.
Proverbs 11:15	One who is a guarantor for a stranger will certainly suffer for it, but one who hates being a guarantor is secure.
Proverbs 17:18	A person lacking in sense shakes hands and becomes guarantor in the presence of his neighbor.
Proverbs 22:26	Do not be among those who shake hands, among those who become guarantors for debts.
	Verses about Lending
Exodus 22:25	"If you lend money to My people, to the poor among you, you are not to act as a creditor to him; you shall not charge him interest." [*Moses is speaking.*]
Deuteronomy 15:7–11	"If there is a poor person among you, one of your brothers, in any of your towns in your land which the LORD your God is giving you, you shall not harden your heart, nor close your hand from your poor brother; but you shall fully open your hand to him, and generously lend him enough for his need *in* whatever he lacks. Be careful that there is no mean-spirited thought in your heart, such as, 'The seventh year, the year of release of debts, is near,' and

	your eye is malicious toward your poor brother, and you give him nothing; then he may cry out to the LORD against you, and it will be a sin in you. You shall generously give to him, and your heart shall not be grudging when you give to him, because for this thing the LORD your God will bless you in all your work, and in all your undertakings. For the poor will not cease to exist in the land; therefore I am commanding you, saying, 'You shall fully open your hand to your brother, to your needy and poor in your land.'" [*Moses is speaking.*]
Deuteronomy 23:19–20	"You are not to charge interest to your countrymen: interest on money, food, or anything that may be loaned on interest. You may charge interest to a foreigner, but to your countrymen you shall not charge interest, so that the LORD your God may bless you in all that you undertake in the land which you are about to enter to possess." [*Moses is speaking.*]
Psalm 37:25–26	I have been young and now I am old, yet I have not seen the righteous forsaken or his descendants begging for bread. All day long he is gracious and lends, and his descendants are a blessing.
Psalm 112:5	It *goes* well for a person who is gracious and lends; he will maintain his cause in judgment.

| Matthew 5:42 | "Give to him who asks of you, and do not turn away from him who wants to borrow from you." [*Jesus is speaking.*] |
| Luke 6:35 | "But love your enemies and do good, and lend, expecting nothing in return; and your reward will be great, and you will be sons of the Most High; for He Himself is kind to ungrateful and evil *people*." [*Jesus is speaking.*] |

REAL-LIFE APPLICATION

Steve was proud that he had been able to pay off his credit card in full each month, thereby avoiding interest payments. He had no other debts, so he was debt-free! He was now considering buying a house and was concerned about being able to save enough for a significant downpayment in a quickly appreciating housing market. He did have enough for a small downpayment, but was worried about needing to get a larger mortgage. After consulting his financial advisor he realized that this would be ok for an appreciating asset like a house, as long as the payments were affordable and he could handle all the home ownership costs. He was excited about this, and happy that his high credit score would help him get the best interest rate on a mortgage.

QUESTIONS

1. What does the Bible say about getting into debt to others here on earth? Does being in debt to someone affect your ability to love them?

2. If you are in debt, how does that make you feel? Are you worried about being able to make payments? Does this limit your financial flexibility or giving?

3. If you are in debt, what is the Bible's advice regarding getting out of debt?

4. Have you ever cosigned for a child or a friend or considered doing so? Did you know that there were Bible verses about cosigning? What are your thoughts on this?

5. How do these verses on lending affect your views regarding lending money to family and friends? What is your attitude about being repaid if you lend to others?

Chapter 8

WEALTH

God is clearly not opposed to wealth, as He made some people in the Old Testament very wealthy. This included Abraham, Isaac, Joseph, David, Solomon, and Job. The focus is more on recognizing the source of wealth and having the right attitude regarding wealth.

BIBLE VERSES	
	Verses about People God Blessed with Wealth
Genesis 24:34-35 (ESV)	So he said, "I am Abraham's servant. The LORD has greatly blessed my master, and he has become great. He has given him flocks and herds, silver and gold, male servants and female servants, camels and donkeys."
Genesis 26:12–13	Now Isaac sowed in that land and reaped in the same year a hundred times *as much*. And the LORD blessed him, and the man became rich, and continued to grow richer until he became very wealthy.

Genesis 41:38–40	Then Pharaoh said to his servants, "Can we find a man like this, in whom there is a divine spirit?" So Pharaoh said to Joseph, "Since God has informed you of all this, there is no one as discerning and wise as you are. You shall be in charge of my house, and all my people shall be obedient to you; only *regarding* the throne will I be greater than you."
2 Samuel 5:10	David became greater and greater, for the LORD God of armies was with him.
1 Kings 3:9–13	"So give Your servant an understanding heart to judge Your people, to discern between good and evil. For who is capable of judging this great people of Yours?" Now it was pleasing in the sight of the Lord that Solomon had asked this thing. And God said to him, "Because you have asked this thing, and have not asked for yourself a long life, nor have asked riches for yourself, nor have you asked for the lives of your enemies, but have asked for yourself discernment to understand justice, behold, I have done according to your words. Behold, I have given you a wise and discerning heart, so that there has been no one like you before you, nor shall one like you arise after you. I have also given you what you have not asked, both riches and honor, so that there will not be any among the kings like you all your days."
Job 1:1–3	There was a man in the land of Uz whose name was Job; and that man was blameless, upright, fearing God and turning away from

	evil. Seven sons and three daughters were born to him. His possessions were seven thousand sheep, three thousand camels, five hundred yoke of oxen, five hundred female donkeys, and very many servants; and that man was the greatest of all the men of the east.
Job 42:10	The LORD also restored the fortunes of Job when he prayed for his friends, and the LORD increased double all that Job had.
	Verses about Having Wealth
Deuteronomy 8:17–19	"Otherwise, you may say in your heart, 'My power and the strength of my hand made me this wealth.' But you are to remember the LORD your God, for it is He who is giving you power to make wealth, in order to confirm His covenant which He swore to your fathers, as *it is* this day. And it shall come about, if you ever forget the LORD your God and follow other gods and serve and worship them, I testify against you today that you will certainly perish." [*Moses is speaking.*]
Psalm 35:27 (ESV)	Let those who delight in my righteousness shout for joy and be glad and say evermore, "Great is the LORD, who delights in the welfare of his servant!"
Proverbs 8:17–21	"I love those who love me; and those who diligently seek me will find me. Riches and honor are with me, enduring wealth and

	righteousness. My fruit is better than gold, even pure gold; and my yield *better* than choice silver. I walk in the way of righteousness, in the midst of the paths of justice, to endow those who love me with wealth, that I may fill their treasuries." [*Wisdom is speaking, as personified by Solomon.*]
Proverbs 10:22	It is the blessings of the LORD that makes rich, and He adds no sorrow to it.
Proverbs 11:28	One who trusts in his riches will fall, but the righteous will flourish like the *green* leaf.
Proverbs 15:6 (ESV)	In the house of the righteous there is much treasure, but trouble befalls the income of the wicked.
Proverbs 21:20	There is precious treasure and oil in the home of the wise, but a foolish person swallows it up.
Proverbs 22:4	The reward of humility and the fear of the LORD are riches, honor, and life.
Proverbs 23:4 (ESV)	Do not toil to acquire wealth; be discerning enough to desist.
Ecclesiastes 5:13	There is a sickening evil *which* I have seen under the sun: wealth being hoarded by its owner to his detriment.
Ecclesiastes 5:18–19	Here is what I have seen to be good and fitting: to eat, to drink, and enjoy oneself in all one's labor in which he labors under the sun *during*

	the few years of his life which God has given him; for this is his reward. Furthermore, as for every person to whom God has given riches and wealth, He has also given him the opportunity to enjoy them and to receive his reward and rejoice in his labor; this is the gift of God.
Matthew 13:18–23 (ESV)	"Hear then the parable of the sower: When anyone hears the word of the kingdom and does not understand it, the evil one comes and snatches away what has been sown in his heart. This is what was sown along the path. As for what was sown in rocky ground, this is the one who hears the word and immediately receives it with joy, yet he has no root in himself, but endures for a while, and when tribulation or persecution arise on account of the word, immediately he falls away. As for what was sown among the thorns, this is the one who hears the word, but the cares of the world and the deceitfulness of riches choke the word, and it proves unfruitful. As for what was sown on good soil, this is the one who hears the word and understands it. He indeed bears fruit and yields, in one case a hundredfold, in another sixty, and in another thirty." [*Jesus is speaking.*]
Luke 12:16–21 (ESV)	And he told them a parable, saying, "The land of a rich man produced plentifully, and he thought to himself, 'What shall I do, for I have nowhere to store my crops?' And he said, 'I will do this: I will tear down my barns and build

	larger ones, and there I will store all my grain and my goods. And I will say to my soul, "Soul, you have ample goods laid up for many years; relax, eat, drink, be merry.'" But God said to him, 'Fool! This night your soul is required of you, and the things you have prepared, whose will they be?' So is the one who lays up treasure for himself and is not rich toward God." [*Jesus is speaking.*]
2 Corinthians 5:10	For we must all appear before the judgement seat of Christ, so that each one may receive compensation for his deeds *done* through the body, in accordance with what he has done, whether good or bad
1 Timothy 6:17–19	Instruct those who are rich in this present world not to be conceited or to set their hope on the uncertainty of riches, but on God, who richly supplies us with all things to enjoy. *Instruct them* to do good, to be rich in good works, to be generous and ready to share, storing up for themselves the treasure of a good foundation for the future, so that they may take hold of that which is truly life.
James 1:5	But if any of you lacks wisdom, let him ask of God, who gives to all generously and without reproach, and it will be given to him.
James 1:17	Every good thing given and every perfect gift is from above, coming down from the Father of lights, with whom there is no variation or shifting shadow.

| 1 John 2:15–17 (ESV) | Do not love the world or the things in the world. If anyone loves the world, the love of the Father is not in him. For all that is in the world—the desires of the flesh and the desires of the eyes and the pride of life—is not from the Father but is from the world. And the world is passing away along with its desires, but whoever does the will of God abides forever. |

REAL-LIFE APPLICATION

Tyrell and Tamika had been blessed financially and enjoyed living very comfortably but never felt that attached to money or their possessions. They had more than they needed, and they were happy to share. This included generously giving to their church and other ministries. When they needed to move into an assisted living facility, they wanted to find other people who would enjoy the furniture and other things they had in their home. So they gave everything away to people in need and to young people just getting started living in their own apartments. They will always treasure the joy they saw in the recipients.

QUESTIONS

1. What is your attitude toward wealth? Are there areas in which God has blessed you? Make a list below.

2. What does the Bible tell people who have wealth to do? And what does it say not to do?

3. How do you feel God is calling you to use the wealth that you have been blessed with?

4. Do you think God wants you to spend some of your wealth for your enjoyment? If yes, how do you decide how much to spend for your enjoyment? Make a list of things that come to mind.

Chapter 9

SAVING AND INVESTING

The Bible is consistent in saying that the right way to build wealth is to work hard, to be diligent, to have integrity, and to spend wisely. It also supports the importance of investing and diversifying.

BIBLE VERSES	
Proverbs 10:4	Poor is one who works with a lazy hand, but the hand of the diligent makes rich.
Proverbs 13:11 (ESV)	Wealth gained hastily will dwindle, but whoever gathers little by little will increase it.
Proverbs 14:23–24	In all labor there is profit, but mere talk *leads* only to poverty. The crown of the wise is their riches, *but* the foolishness of fools is *simply* foolishness.
Proverbs 15:27 (ESV)	Whoever is greedy for unjust gain troubles his own household, but he who hates bribes will live.

Proverbs 21:5	The plans of the diligent certainly *lead* to advantage, but everyone who is in a hurry certainly *comes* to poverty.
Proverbs 21:17	One who loves pleasure *will* become a poor person; one who loves wine and oil will not become rich.
Proverbs 27:12	A prudent person sees evil *and* hides himself; *but* the naïve proceed, *and* pay the penalty.
Proverbs 28:20	A faithful person will abound with blessings, but one who hurries to be rich will not go unpunished.
Proverbs 28:22 (ESV)	A stingy man hastens after wealth and does not know that poverty will come upon him.
Ecclesiastes 11:2	Divide your portion to seven, or even to eight, for you do not know what misfortune may occur on the earth.
Matthew 25:24–27 (ESV)	"He also who had received the one talent came forward, saying, 'Master, I knew you to be a hard man, reaping where you did not sow, and gathering where you scattered no seed, so I was afraid and I went and hid your talent in the ground. Here, you have what is yours.' But his master answered him, 'You wicked and slothful servant! You knew that I reap where I have not sown and gather where I scattered no seed? Then you ought to have invested my money with the bankers, and at my coming I should have received what was my own with interest.'" [*Jesus is speaking.*]

1 Timothy 6:9–10	But those who want to get rich fall into temptation and a trap, and many foolish and harmful desires which plunge people into ruin and destruction. For the love of money is a root of all sorts of evil, and some by longing for it have wandered away from the faith and pierced themselves with many griefs.

Verses about Having Counselors

Proverbs 5:23	He will die for lack of instruction, and in the greatness of his foolishness he will go astray.
Proverbs 11:14	Where there is no guidance the people fall, but in an abundance of counselors there is victory.
Proverbs 15:22	Without consultation, plans are frustrated, but with many counselors they succeed.

REAL-LIFE APPLICATION

Peter had paid off his debt and was looking forward to starting to save. He heard about people who were making a lot of money by investing in Bitcoin, and this piqued his interest. Thankfully, he learned that Bitcoin is a highly speculative market with a lot of volatility and decided not to do this. After consulting the Bible and talking to his financial advisor, he decided that investing in a moderate allocation mutual fund that had a diversified portfolio of stocks and bonds would be a good solution for him based on his age, his risk tolerance, and biblical guidance. He felt that ongoing investments in this mutual fund would be a good way to benefit from market growth while limiting his risk.

QUESTIONS

1. Some people say that the Bible says money is the root of all evil, but 1 Timothy 6:10 actually says "For the love of money is a root of all sorts of evil". What is the difference, and how does this affect investing?

2. What is your approach toward investing? Do you take big risks, hoping to realize quick gains? Would you describe your investing style as aggressive, moderate, or conservative? Make a list of your main investments (home, mutual funds, ETFs, stocks, bonds, cash, etc.).

3. Are you saving enough of the proceeds from your labors (working and investing) in order to build the wealth you need to live, support your family, and give generously for the rest of your life? List the key elements of your plan below.

4. Do you have people giving you advice regarding saving and investing? Are you confident that they can give you good, biblically-based advice?

Chapter 10

CONTENTMENT

Contentment with money, possessions, and financial circumstances can be a challenge regardless of whether someone is poor or rich (in worldly terms). The Bible encourages and challenges us to consider the motives behind any lack of contentment we may feel and to be content. However, this is not easy! Read the verses below and discern how this applies to you.

BIBLE VERSES	
Proverbs 30:7–9	Two things I have asked of You; do not refuse me before I die: keep deception and lies far from me, give me neither poverty nor riches; feed me with the food that is my portion, so that I will not be full and deny You and say "Who is the LORD?" and that I will not become impoverished and steal, and profane the name of my God.
Ecclesiastes 5:10	One who loves money will not be satisfied with money, nor one who loves abundance *with its* income. This too is futility.

Ecclesiastes 5:15	As he came naked from his mother's womb, so he will return as he came. He will take nothing from the fruit of his labor that he can carry in his hand.
Matthew 6:25–27 (ESV)	"Therefore I tell you, do not be anxious about your life, what you will eat or what you will drink, nor about your body, what you will put on. Is not life more than food, and the body more than clothing? Look at the birds of the air: they neither sow nor reap nor gather into barns, and yet your heavenly Father feeds them. Are you not of more value than they? And which of you by being anxious can add a single hour to his span of life?" [*Jesus is speaking.*]
Matthew 16:26	"For what good will it do a person if he gains the whole world, but forfeits his soul? Or what will a person give in exchange for his soul?" [*Jesus is speaking.*]
Luke 12:15	But He said to them, "Beware, and be on your guard against every form of greed; for not *even* when one is affluent does his life consist of his possessions." [*Jesus is speaking.*]
Philippians 3:7	But whatever things were gain to me, these things I have counted as loss because of Christ.
Philippians 4:11–13	Not that I speak from need, for I have learned to be content in whatever *circumstances* I am. I know how to get along with little, and I also

	know how to live in prosperity; in any and every *circumstance* I have learned the secret of being filled and going hungry, both of having abundance and suffering need. I can do all things through Him who strengthens me.
Colossians 3:15–17	Let the peace of Christ, to which you were indeed called in one body, rule in your hearts; and be thankful. Let the word of Christ richly dwell within you, with all wisdom teaching and admonishing one another with psalms, hymns, *and* spiritual songs, singing with thankfulness in your hearts to God. Whatever you do in word or deed, *do* everything in the name of the Lord Jesus, giving thanks through Him to God the Father.
2 Thessalonians 2:16–17	Now may our Lord Jesus Christ Himself and God our Father, who has loved us and given us eternal comfort and good hope by grace, comfort and strengthen your hearts in every good work and word.
1 Timothy 4:4–5	For everything created by God is good, and nothing is to be rejected if it is received with gratitude; for it is sanctified by means of the word of God and prayer.
1 Timothy 6:6–8 (ESV)	But godliness with contentment is great gain, for we brought nothing into the world, and we cannot take anything out of the world. But if we have food and clothing, with these we will be content.

Hebrews 13:5 (ESV)	Keep your life free from love of money, and be content with what you have, for he has said, "I will never leave you nor forsake you." [*God is speaking.*]
James 3:16–17	For where jealousy and selfish ambition exist, there is disorder and every evil thing. But the wisdom from above is first pure, then peace-loving, gentle, reasonable, full of mercy and good fruits, impartial, free of hypocrisy.
James 4:13–16	Come now, you who say, "Today or tomorrow we will go to such and such a city, and spend a year there and engage in business and make a profit." Yet you do not know what your life will be like tomorrow. For you are *just* a vapor that appears for a little while, and then vanishes away. Instead, *you ought* to say, "If the Lord wills, we will live and also do this or that." But as it is, you boast in your arrogance; all such boasting is evil. [*James is speaking about what business people say.*]

REAL-LIFE APPLICATION

Kathy grew up in a middle-class family and had all she needed, but she was always jealous of the other girls in her high school who came from wealthier families and were able to have nice cars and more fashionable clothes. During her senior year, she went on a mission trip to Central America that totally changed her perspective. She saw people there who were very poor while at the same time being very happy. This puzzled her at first. However, she came to realize that the reason was that they had close-knit families who loved each other, that the people in the community they lived in supported each other, and that material possessions just weren't a priority. They were satisfied with what they had and focused on relationships. She also learned that they were very religious and trusted God to provide. This was very different from her town, where people were very focused on possessions and wanted to trust only themselves. When she came home, Kathy was a different person. She was much more supportive and loving with her family and friends. She also learned to be content with what she had, which was more like the people she had been with in Central America.

QUESTIONS

1. Are there areas in which you are not content with your money, possessions, and standard of living? Make a list below.

2. What are the reasons why you are discontented? Are you envious of what others have? Are you anxious that you don't have enough for you and your family to live on? Are there other reasons? Make a list below.

3. Are there ways in which you feel God has blessed you with money and possessions? Make a list below.

4. If you are discontented, what could you do to change your perspective? Are you praying about this? Are there people who are under-resourced that you could support or serve, either directly or through ministries you could get involved with?

5. Should contentment also mean complacency? Or, should you always strive to improve your situation?

Chapter 11

TRUSTING GOD

The Bible encourages us to be content with our financial situation while appropriately striving to improve it. However, it is more important to realize that we can trust God with our lives and our future. The Bible encourages us to be confident, knowing that we are saved, can trust in the Lord, and will ultimately reside with Him in heaven.

BIBLE VERSES	
Psalm 100:1–5 (ESV)	Make a joyful noise to the LORD, all the earth! Serve the LORD with gladness! Come into his presence with singing! Know that the LORD, he is God! It is he who made us, and we are his; we are his people, and the sheep of his pasture. Enter his gates with thanksgiving, and his courts with praise! Give thanks to him; bless his name! For the LORD is good; his steadfast love endures forever, and his faithfulness to all generations.
Proverbs 3:5–7	Trust in the LORD with all your heart and do not lean on your own understanding. In all your ways acknowledge Him, and He will make

	your paths straight. Do not be wise in your own eyes; fear the LORD and turn away from evil.
Jeremiah 29:11	"For I know the plans that I have for you," declares the LORD, "plans for prosperity and not for disaster, to give you a future and a hope."
Nahum 1:7	The LORD is good, a stronghold in the day of trouble; and He knows those who take refuge in him.
John 3:16	"For God so loved the world, that He gave his only Son, so that everyone who believes in Him will not perish, but have eternal life." [*Jesus is speaking.*]
Romans 5:8	But God demonstrates His own love toward us, in that while we were still sinners, Christ died for us.
Ephesians 3:20	Now to Him who is able to do far more abundantly beyond all that we ask or think, according to the power at work within us.
Philippians 1:6	*For I am* confident of this very thing, that He who began a good work among you will complete it by the day of Christ Jesus.
Philippians 3:20	For our citizenship is in heaven, from which we also eagerly wait for a Savior, the Lord Jesus Christ.

Philippians 4:4–7	Rejoice in the Lord always; again I will say, rejoice! Let your gentle *spirit* be known to all people. The Lord is near. Do not be anxious about anything, but in everything by prayer and pleading with thanksgiving let your requests be made known to God. And the peace of God, which surpasses all comprehension, will guard your hearts and minds in Christ Jesus.
Colossians 2:13–14	And when you were dead in your wrongdoings and the uncircumcision of your flesh, He made you alive together with Him, having forgiven us all our wrongdoings, having canceled the certificate of debt consisting of decrees against us, which was hostile to us; and He has taken it out of the way, having nailed it to the cross.
1 Thessalonians 5:16–18	Rejoice always, pray without ceasing, in everything give thanks; for this is the will of God for you in Christ Jesus.
Hebrews 6:17–20	In the same way God, desiring even more to demonstrate to the heirs of the promise the fact that His purpose is unchangeable, confirmed it with an oath, so that by two unchangeable things in which it is impossible for God to lie, we who have taken refuge would have strong encouragement to hold firmly to the hope set before us. This hope we have as an anchor of the soul, a *hope* both sure and reliable and one which enters within the veil, where Jesus has entered as a forerunner for us, having become a high priest forever according to the order of Melchizedek.

2 Peter 1:3–4 (ESV)	His divine power has granted to us all things the pertain to life and godliness, through the knowledge of him who called us to his own glory and excellence, by which he has granted to us his precious and very great promises, so that through them you may become partakers of the divine nature, having escaped from the corruption that is in the world because of sinful desire.

REAL-LIFE APPLICATION

When Matt retired, he looked back on his life and reflected on what had brought him the most joy and what he regretted. He realized that the times he had spent with family and helping others in need had brought him the most joy. Some examples were family vacation trips, mission trips to Latin America and Africa, giving to Christian ministries serving the poor, and giving money to friends and family when they urgently needed it. He regretted that his drive for excellence and desire to get ahead had resulted in his being a workaholic, as this detracted from time with his family and led to his not being as close to his adult children as he would like to be. However, looking back, he could also see how God had provided. This included how he met his wife, an unexpected career opportunity that miraculously appeared when his current job was ending, and consistent provision of a good income to support his family. He committed to spending his retirement years being generous, serving others, and being more aware of how much he could trust in God's plan for him and his family. Confidence in God's plan and his eternal security gave him tremendous peace. He wished that he had understood this earlier in life and set different priorities.

QUESTIONS

1. How do you think contentment relates to trusting God?

2. What brings you joy? Are these things based on relationships or money? List some examples.

3. What are your regrets at this stage in your life?

4. Are you trusting God or only trusting in your own abilities?

Chapter 12

IN CLOSING

The Bible clearly has a *lot* to say about money! In fact, so much that it can be difficult to discern what the right balance is between giving (tithing and giving generously to those in need), providing for your family, managing money and investing wisely to build wealth, planning to provide an inheritance, and spending in ways that allow you to enjoy what God has richly blessed you with.

It is also clear that some people have been blessed with more worldly wealth and that God expects these people to share with those who have less and not to solely trust in their possessions. And that they should realize that contentment ultimately depends more on trusting God than money and possessions.

There is no right answer for this balancing act. It depends on what you discern through prayer that God has called you to do and what sacrifices He is calling you to make.

Consider these questions:

1. Do you agree that God owns it all and that we are stewards? What would He want you to do as a good steward?

2. Generosity is a reflection of our obedience to God and our love for others. How do you view yourself?

3. If God has blessed you with wealth or called you to build wealth, are you being generous with it? What are your motivations for doing so or not doing so?

4. Are you experiencing the joy associated with giving to others and serving others?

5. Do you have goals for giving, saving, and spending that are consistent with your beliefs?

6. Are you avoiding consumer debt (e.g., credit card interest payments and car loans), minimizing student loan debt, and managing mortgage payments to an acceptable level?

7.   Are you managing your expenses (giving, saving, and spending) to not exceed your income?

8.   Are you being responsible in how you are protecting and providing for your family?

9.   Are you being disciplined, diligent, and prudent in selecting the best savings accounts and investments?

10. Do you trust that God has a plan for you, are you doing your part, and are you content with His plan?

11. Are you confident in your eternal security?

APPENDIX: LIST OF BIBLE PASSAGES

Old Testament	
Verse(s)	**Chapter(s)**
Genesis 14:18–20	Tithing
Genesis 24:34–35	Wealth
Genesis 26:12–13	Wealth
Genesis 41:34–36	Planning and Budgeting
Genesis 41:38–40	Wealth
Exodus 19:5	Ownership
Exodus 22:25	Debt and Lending
Leviticus 19:10	Caring for the Poor
Leviticus 27:30–33	Tithing
Numbers 18:21	Tithing
Deuteronomy 8:17–19	Wealth
Deuteronomy 10:14	Ownership
Deuteronomy 12: 6–7	Generosity
Deuteronomy 15:7–11	Caring for the Poor; Debt and Lending
Deuteronomy 16:17	Generosity
Deuteronomy 23:19–20	Debt and Lending
Deuteronomy 24:19–21	Caring for the Poor
Deuteronomy 28:12	Debt and Lending
2 Samuel 5:10	Wealth

1 Kings 3:9–13	Wealth
2 Kings 4:1–7	Debt and Lending
1 Chronicles 29:9	Generosity
1 Chronicles 29:11–13	Ownership
2 Chronicles 31:4–5	Tithing
Nehemiah 9:6	Ownership
Nehemiah 13:10–12	Tithing
Job 1:1–3	Wealth
Job 41:11	Ownership
Job 42:10	Wealth
Psalm 24:1–2	Ownership
Psalm 35:27	Wealth
Psalms 37:21	Generosity
Psalm 37:25–26	Debt and Lending
Psalm 50:10–12	Ownership
Psalm 89:11	Ownership
Psalm 100:1–5	Trusting God
Psalm 112:5	Debt and Lending
Proverbs 3:5–7	Trusting God
Proverbs 3:9–10	Tithing
Proverbs 3:13–16	Planning and Budgeting
Proverbs 5:23	Planning and Budgeting; Saving and Investing
Proverbs 6:1–5	Debt and Lending
Proverbs 6:6–8	Planning and Budgeting
Proverbs 8:17–21	Wealth
Proverbs 10:4	Saving and Investing
Proverbs 10:22	Wealth
Proverbs 11:14	Planning and Budgeting; Saving and Investing
Proverbs 11:15	Debt and Lending
Proverbs 11:25	Generosity
Proverbs 11:28	Wealth

Proverbs 13:11	Saving and Investing
Proverbs 13:22	Planning and Budgeting
Proverbs 14:21	Caring for the Poor
Proverbs 14:23–24	Saving and Investing
Proverbs 14:31	Caring for the Poor
Proverbs 15:6	Wealth
Proverbs 15:22	Planning and Budgeting; Saving and Investing
Proverbs 15:27	Saving and Investing
Proverbs 17:18	Debt and Lending
Proverbs 19:14	Planning and Budgeting
Proverbs 19:17	Caring for the Poor
Proverbs 19:21	Planning and Budgeting
Proverbs 21:5	Planning and Budgeting; Saving and Investing
Proverbs 21:13	Caring for the Poor
Proverbs 21:17	Saving and Investing
Proverbs 21:20	Planning and Budgeting; Wealth
Proverbs 22:4	Wealth
Proverbs 22:7	Debt and Lending
Proverbs 22:9	Caring for the Poor
Proverbs 22:16	Caring for the Poor
Proverbs 22:26	Debt and Lending
Proverbs 23:4	Wealth
Proverbs 24:3–4	Planning and Budgeting
Proverbs 24:27	Planning and Budgeting
Proverbs 27:12	Saving and Investing
Proverbs 27:23–24	Planning and Budgeting
Proverbs 28:20	Saving and Investing
Proverbs 28:22	Saving and Investing
Proverbs 28:27	Caring for the Poor
Proverbs 30:7–9	Contentment

Proverbs 30:24–25	Planning and Budgeting
Ecclesiastes 5:10	Contentment
Ecclesiastes 5:13	Wealth
Ecclesiastes 5:15	Contentment
Ecclesiastes 5:18–19	Wealth
Ecclesiastes 11:2	Saving and Investing
Jeremiah 29:11	Trusting God
Ezekiel 16:49	Caring for the Poor
Nahum 1:7	Trusting God
Malachi 3:8–11	Tithing

New Testament	
Verse(s)	**Chapter(s)**
Matthew 5:42	Debt and Lending
Matthew 6:3–4	Caring for the Poor
Matthew 6:19–21	Generosity
Matthew 6:24	Stewardship
Matthew 6:25–27	Contentment
Matthew 7:12	Generosity
Matthew 7:24–27	Planning and Budgeting
Matthew 13:18–23	Wealth
Matthew 16:26	Contentment
Matthew 19:21–26	Caring for the Poor
Matthew 22:36–40	Generosity
Matthew 23:23	Tithing
Matthew 25:19–30	Stewardship
Matthew 25:24–27	Saving and Investing
Matthew 25:34–40	Caring for the Poor
Mark 12:41–44	Generosity
Luke 6:35	Debt and Lending
Luke 6:38	Generosity
Luke 10:36–37	Caring for the Poor
Luke 12:15	Contentment
Luke 12:16–21	Wealth

Luke 12:42–48	Stewardship
Luke 14:12–14	Caring for the Poor
Luke 14:28–30	Planning and Budgeting
Luke 16:10–13	Stewardship
John 3:16	Trusting God
Acts 17:24–25	Ownership
Acts 20:35	Generosity
Romans 5:8	Trusting God
Romans 13:7	Planning and Budgeting
Romans 13:8	Debt and Lending
1 Corinthians 4:2	Stewardship
1 Corinthians 10:26	Ownership
2 Corinthians 5:10	Wealth
2 Corinthians 8:1–4	Generosity
2 Corinthians 9:6–11	Generosity
2 Corinthians 12:14	Planning and Budgeting
Galatians 6:6	Tithing
Ephesians 3:20	Trusting God
Philippians 1:6	Trusting God
Philippians 3:7	Contentment
Philippians 3:20	Trusting God
Philippians 4:4–7	Trusting God
Philippians 4:11–13	Contentment
Philippians 4:16–19	Generosity
Colossians 1:15–17	Ownership
Colossians 2:13–14	Trusting God
Colossians 3:15–17	Contentment
Colossians 3:23	Planning and Budgeting
1 Thessalonians 5:16–18	Trusting God
2 Thessalonians 2:16–17	Contentment
1 Timothy 4:4–5	Contentment
1 Timothy 5:3–4	Planning and Budgeting
1 Timothy 5:8	Planning and Budgeting

1 Timothy 5:16	Planning and Budgeting
1 Timothy 5:17–18	Tithing
1 Timothy 6:6–8	Contentment
1 Timothy 6:9–10	Saving and Investing
1 Timothy 6:17–19	Generosity; Wealth
2 Timothy 3:16–17	Introduction
Hebrews 6:17–20	Trusting God
Hebrews 13:2	Generosity
Hebrews 13:5	Contentment
Hebrews 13:16	Generosity
James 1:5	Wealth
James 1:17	Wealth
James 1:27	Caring for the Poor
James 3:16–17	Contentment
James 4:13–16	Contentment
2 Peter 1:3–4	Trusting God
1 John 2:15–17	Wealth
1 John 3:16–18	Caring for the Poor
Revelation 4:11	Ownership

ABOUT THE AUTHOR

Greg Huber has been a follower of Jesus for more than forty years and has held various church leadership positions. He's always understood what the Bible says about giving money to the church, but he didn't hear much about what it says about other areas of money management.

After founding a small Christian financial planning ministry, he realized that the Bible offers tremendous financial wisdom for many other aspects of life as well. Greg wants to enable Christians to make better financial decisions and be more content by understanding what the Bible teaches about money and by integrating this into their lives.

Printed in the United States
by Baker & Taylor Publisher Services